Level 4 Diploma in Accounting

Credit Management and Debt Control

First edition 2010
Third edition 2012

ISBN 9781 4453 9482 4 (Previous edition 9780 7517 9754 1)

British Library Cataloguing-in-Publication Data

A catalogue record for this book is available from the British Library

Published by

BPP Learning Media Ltd, BPP House, Aldine Place, London W12 8AA

www.bpp.com/learningmedia

Printed in the United Kingdom

Your learning materials, published by BPP Learning Media Ltd,
are printed on paper sourced from sustainable, managed forests.

Welcome to BPP Learning Media's AAT **Passcards for Credit Management and Debt Control**.

- They **save you time**. Important topics are summarised for you.

- They incorporate **diagrams** to kick start your memory.

- They follow the overall **structure** of the BPP Texts, but BPP Learning Media's AAT **Passcards** are not just a condensed book. Each card has been separately designed for clear presentation. Topics are self-contained and can be grasped visually.

- AAT **Passcards** are still **just the right size** for pockets, briefcases and bags.

- AAT **Passcards focus on the assessment** you will be facing.

- AAT **Passcards focus on the essential points** that you need to know in the workplace, or when completing your computer based assessment.

Run through the complete set of **Passcards** as often as you can during your final revision period. The day before the assessment, try to go through the **Passcards** again! You will then be well on your way to completing the assessment successfully.

Good luck!

The BPP **Question Bank** contains activities and assessments that provide invaluable practice in the skills you need to complete this unit successfully.

1: Managing the granting of credit

Topic List

Liquidity

Credit control

Assessment of credit status

This chapter serves as a general introduction to credit management and control which will be considered in more detail later.

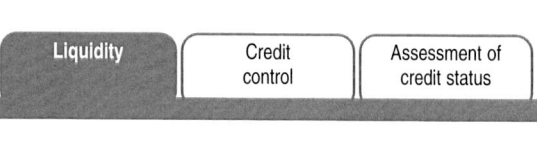

Liquidity

- Ability to pay amounts when due

- Inventory + receivables – payables

- Also cash/bank balances and short-term investments

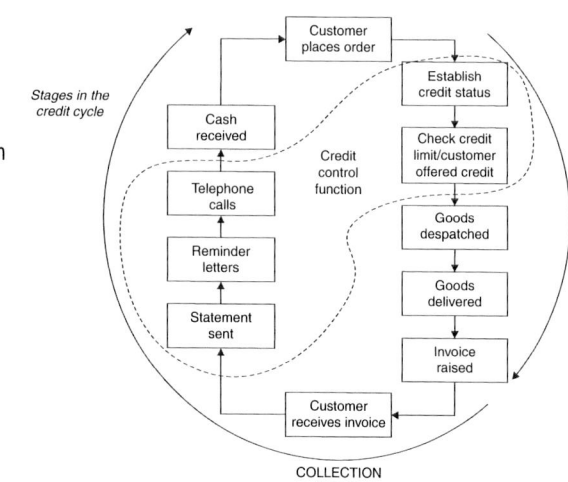

CREDIT CONTROL POLICIES

Overall terms

- No credit at all?
- Credit only to particular classes of customer
- Total credit offered is X% of turnover

Procedures for offering credit

- Obtaining references
- Reviewing account information
- Customer visits
- Formal agreement
  - Complies with consumer credit legislation
  - Probationary period
  - Settlement terms

Control

- Aged receivables analysis
- Chasing slow payers

Credit risk means that there is a possibility that the debt will become irrecoverable. A **credit assessment** is a judgement about the creditworthiness of a customer, providing a basis for a decision as to whether credit should be

HIGH

↑

Unacceptable risk

Customers responsible for most irrecoverable debt problems but can generate high revenue

Customers who exploit trade credit in full/overseas customers who have difficulty remitting payments

Customers with good reputation and no history of payment problems

Zero or negligible risk (government institutions and major companies)

↓

LOW

Remember!

Credit assessment will not only be needed when credit is first granted, but also when customers request higher limits or their volume of trade takes them above their existing limits.

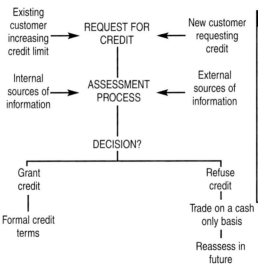

Internal information		External information
	REQUEST FOR CREDIT	
Existing customer increasing credit limit →		← New customer requesting credit
■ Staff knowledge	ASSESSMENT PROCESS	■ Bank reference
■ Customer visits		■ Trade reference
■ Financial analysis of customer accounts	Internal sources of information → ← External sources of information	■ Credit reference agencies
	DECISION?	■ Companies House
		■ Media publications
		■ Internet
		■ Management accounts from customer

Grant credit

Refuse credit

Formal credit terms

Trade on a cash only basis

Reassess in future

Notes

2: Granting credit to customers

Topic List

References

Ratio analysis

Credit scoring

Using credit control information

This chapter takes you through the assessment of the reliability of potential credit customers. It summarises the sources of information you can use when making the assessment. You will certainly have to demonstrate that you can use evidence about potential customers to make sensible recommendations which are in line with your organisation's credit control policies.

Bank references

Should ask in precise terms eg 'Do you consider X Ltd to be good for trade credit of £1,000 per month on terms of 30 days?'

Trade references

Remember!

- Customer may maintain untypically good relations with referees.
- Referee should be offering similar terms.
- Referee may be connected or influenced by potential customer.
- Unknown company's reference should be treated with caution.
- References should be followed up.

Types of bank reference

- Undoubted   **BEST**
- Considered good for your purposes
- Should prove good for your figures
- Well constituted business whose capital would appear to be fully employed; we do not think directors/shareholders would undertake something they felt they could not fulfil
- Unable to speak for your figures   **WORST**

Credit reference agencies provide information about businesses so that their creditworthiness can be assessed by suppliers.

☑ Summary of information	☒ May not contain up-to-date information
☑ Means of cross-checking other information	☒ Suppliers' references are out-of-date
	☒ Lack of information on new businesses

Contents of agency report

- Legal data
- Commercial data
- Credit data

Other information

- Press
- Historical, financial data
- Management accounts
- Companies' Registry search
- County Court records
- Internet search
- Credit circles

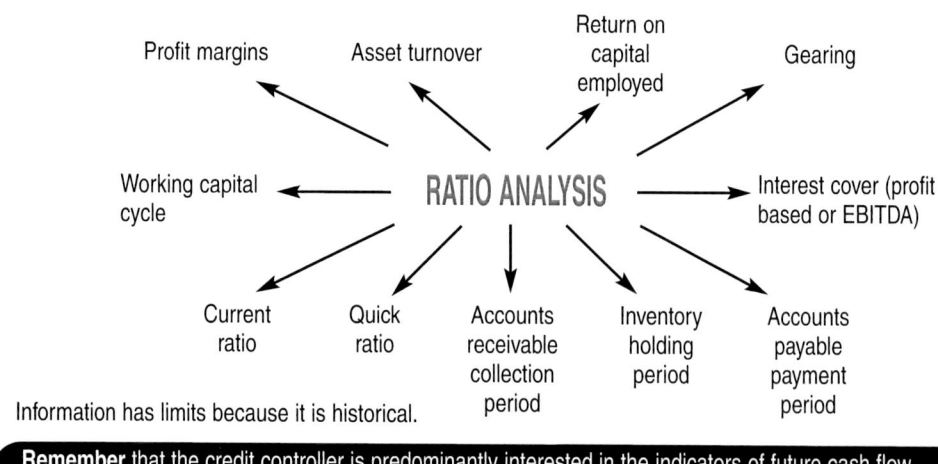

Information has limits because it is historical.

Remember that the credit controller is predominantly interested in the indicators of future cash flow (liquidity, gearing, working capital).

Credit scoring is a method of assessing the creditworthiness of an individual or organisation using statistical analysis. It is used by banks, utility companies, insurance companies and landlords to assess the ability of an individual or organisation to repay any loans or pay for goods and services.

Factors considered

- Financials
- Business details
- Publicly available data
- Payment record
- Owners
- Economic index

Example

Operating profit margin	X
Interest cover	X
Liquidity ratio	X
Gearing	X
Credit score	**X**

The old AAT practice assessment contains an example of a credit scoring system.

2: Granting credit to customers

Credit control information should be used in various ways.

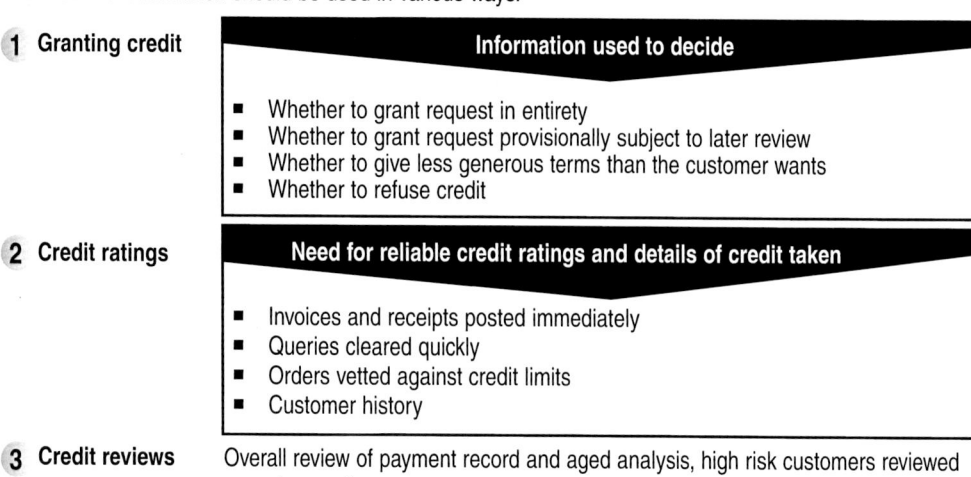

1 Granting credit

Information used to decide

- Whether to grant request in entirety
- Whether to grant request provisionally subject to later review
- Whether to give less generous terms than the customer wants
- Whether to refuse credit

2 Credit ratings

Need for reliable credit ratings and details of credit taken

- Invoices and receipts posted immediately
- Queries cleared quickly
- Orders vetted against credit limits
- Customer history

3 Credit reviews Overall review of payment record and aged analysis, high risk customers reviewed more frequently

Opening new account: Business name
Contact name & title
Business address & phone no.
Credit limit
Payment terms

Reasons for refusal of credit

- Poor bank reference
- Poor trade references
- Concerns re validity of trade references
- Adverse press comment
- Poor credit agency report
- Info from credit circle
- Poor financial analysis
- Newly started business so no track record

Communication

- Polite and tactful
- Explanation of reasons
- Trading on cash terms
- Future reassessment of credit worthiness
- Follow up call

Notes

3: Legislation and credit control

Topic List

Contract law

Bankruptcy and insolvency

Other legislation

Data protection

Bringing a court action

In this chapter we consider the ways in which a variety of legislation impacts upon the credit control function. The main areas are those of contract law and breaches of contract but we will also consider other areas of legislation which are important.

A **contract** is an agreement which legally binds the parties (offeror and offeree).

Validity of a contract affected by:

- Content – complete and precise
- Form – certain contracts in precise form
- Genuine consent
- Legality
- Capacity – some parties have restricted capacity

Defective contracts

- Void – no contract
- Voidable – parties can terminate
- Unenforceable – parties need not perform

Essential elements of a contract

- Offer and acceptance = Agreement
- Value/consideration (what price in exchange for promise)
- Intention to create legal relations

Offer

- Invitation to treat (advert catalogue, price ticket)
- Verbal or written
- Duration – set term or reasonable
- Revocation – offer cancelled
- Counter offer – amounts to rejection
- Acceptance – valid acceptance (written or verbal) ends offer

Contract terms

Express   – Specifically stated

Conditions   – Fundamental terms
              – Breach of contract if broken

Warranties   – Less important terms
              – Contract not terminated if broken

Implied   – Not stated but implied by trade custom
                or law

Breach of contract
When one of the parties fails to perform. Remedies: ■ Action for the price (recovery of agreed sum)   ■ Damages (compensation for loss)   ■ Termination   ■ Specific performance   ■ *Quantum meruit* (value for work done)   ■ Injunction

Bankruptcy is the legal status of an *individual* against whom an order has been made by the court because of an inability to meet financial liabilities.

Creditors demand payment and petition for bankruptcy.

Individual cannot dispose of property/settle legal claims.

Official appointed to investigate/realise assets.

Assets realised and creditors paid in order of preference.

Insolvency is the inability of a *company* to pay its debts when they fall due.

Company may suffer **liquidation/winding-up** (similar procedures to bankruptcy) or receivership (receiver appointed to obtain money by realising assets).

Company may be able to use alternative procedures (**administration, voluntary arrangements**) depending on legal jurisdiction to keep going.

Sale of goods

Sale of Goods Acts govern sale of goods. Key conditions:

- Title passes on delivery even if payment delayed
- Title passes on sale or return goods when buyer accepts
- If conditions imposed, must be fulfilled
- Key necessities: satisfactory quality, fit for purpose, as described

Other legislation

- Trade Descriptions Act
- Unfair Contract Terms Act
- Consumer Credit Act
- Late Payment of Commercial Debts (Interest) Act

Failure to pay

- Goods stopped in transit
- Lien by seller if goods not passed
- Retention of title clauses

Interest = gross debt × (Bank of England base rate + 8%) × number of days late/365

Data Protection Act 1998

Aims to protect individuals (data subjects).

Definitions

Personal information – held about living individual, factual and expressions of opinion
Data subject – individual for whom data held
Data controller – person who holds + processes personal information

- Data subjects have certain legal rights.

- Data controller must notify the Information Commissioner annually that they are processing personal information.

- Data controller must follow data protection principles of good practice.

Data protection

- Apply to paper-based/microfilm/microfiche systems as well as computer systems
- Conditions under which fair processing of personal information prescribed
- Processing of personal information forbidden unless certain conditions apply
- Processing of sensitive (racial, political, religious) information forbidden without consent
- Data subjects must be told reasons for data processing

Seven rights of data subjects

- Right to subject access
- Right to prevent processing
- Right to prevent processing for direct marketing
- Rights in relation to automated decision making
- Right to compensation
- Right to rectification, blocking, erasure + destruction
- Right to ask commissioner to assess if Act contravened

Court action

Before taking action, check:

- Genuine debt not dissatisfied customer
- Exact identity of receivable
- Receivable's financial resources

The amount owed, type of transaction, and public interest issues will determine court used.

< £5,000	Small claims
£5,000–25,000	County Court (fast track)
> £25,000	County Court (multitrack) or High Court

Court enforcement

- Deductions from wages (attachment of earnings order)
- Redirection of payments from third party (garnishee order)
- Seizure of goods (warrant of execution)
- Administrative order
- Receiver
- Restriction on assets (legal charge)
- Insolvency procedures

4: Methods of credit control

Topic List

Settlement discounts

Methods of debt collection

In this chapter we will consider a variety of ways of encouraging receivables to pay the amounts due ranging from the use of settlement discounts to the use of external parties.

Advantages of settlement discounts

- Encourage customer to pay earlier and thus reduce financing costs
- Improve liquidity
- Encourage customers to buy

Cost of settlement discount

$$\left(\frac{d}{100 - d} \times \frac{365}{N - D} \right) \times 100\%$$

where

d is discount percentage offered

N is the number of days credit offered net, for no discount

D is the number of days credit allowed with settlement discount

Example

Henry Ltd offers with no discount three months credit. The company is considering a 5% discount to all customers paying within one month.

$$\text{Cost of early settlement discount} = \left(\frac{5}{100 - 5} \times \frac{365}{90 - 30} \right) \times 100\% = 32\%$$

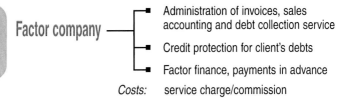

Factoring is debt collection by factor company which advances proportion of money due. It can be with or without recourse.

Factor company

- Administration of invoices, sales accounting and debt collection service
- Credit protection for client's debts
- Factor finance, payments in advance

Costs: service charge/commission
interest charge on amounts outstanding

Benefits of factoring finance

- Pay suppliers promptly
- Maintain optimum inventory levels
- Growth financed through sales rather than external capital
- Factor will chase slow payers
- Finance linked to volume of sales

However use of a factor may give a negative image of the organisation to the customer.

Invoice discounting is the sale of debts for discount in return for cash. The receivable is unaware of the discounter's involvement and continues to pay the supplier.

Debt insurance

- Whole turnover policy
- Annual aggregate excess policy
- Specific receivables

Debt collection agencies

Agencies receive a percentage of debts collected. Some collect on letter/telephone basis, others collect on the doorstep.

5: Managing the supply of credit

Topic List

Aged receivables' listing

Irrecoverable debts

Collecting debts

When managing receivables it is important to monitor balances outstanding on a regular basis and then to follow the organisation's policies in the chasing and collection of these debts.

| Aged receivables' listing | Irrecoverable debts | Collecting debts |

Aged receivables' analysis

Account No	Customer name	Balance £	Credit Limit £	Days <30 £	30–60 £	60–90 £	>90 £
1	A	X	X	X	X	X	X
2	B	X	X	X	X	X	X
3	C	X	X	X	X	X	X
4	D	X	X	X	X	X	X

Reports can highlight:

- Overdue accounts
- Slow payers
- Sales revenue and days sales outstanding
- Aggregate for customer classes eg region or industry sector

Important that receivables do not exceed credit limit.

80/20 rule

80% value of amounts owed by customers is represented by 20% of customer accounts.

An **irrecoverable debt** is a debt which is considered to be uncollectable and is written off against profit.

An irrecoverable debt report will give details of when original debt arose and when the debt was written off.

Need to communicate irrecoverable debts to accounting function.

A **doubtful debt** is a debt for which there is some uncertainty as to whether it is irrecoverable.

A **doubtful debt allowance** is an amount charged against profit and deducted from receivables to allow for estimated non-recovery of doubtful debts.

Consider

- Materiality/significance of amount
- Success of attempts to collect debt
- Expenses of pursuing debt
- Likelihood of insolvency proceedings

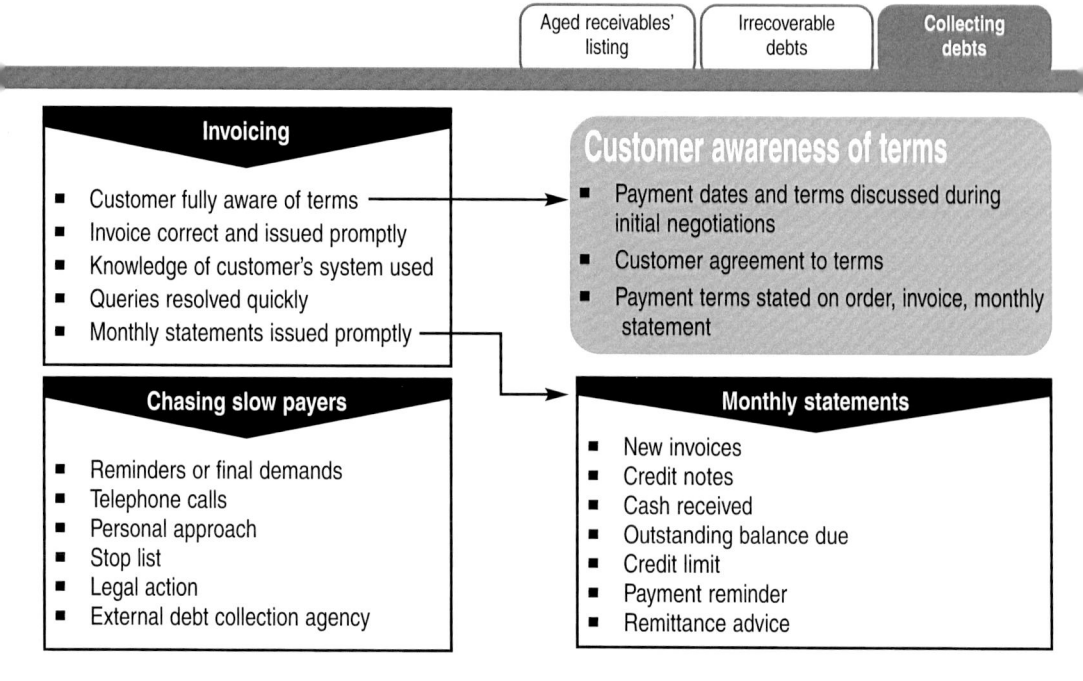

Invoicing

- Customer fully aware of terms
- Invoice correct and issued promptly
- Knowledge of customer's system used
- Queries resolved quickly
- Monthly statements issued promptly

Customer awareness of terms

- Payment dates and terms discussed during initial negotiations
- Customer agreement to terms
- Payment terms stated on order, invoice, monthly statement

Chasing slow payers

- Reminders or final demands
- Telephone calls
- Personal approach
- Stop list
- Legal action
- External debt collection agency

Monthly statements

- New invoices
- Credit notes
- Cash received
- Outstanding balance due
- Credit limit
- Payment reminder
- Remittance advice

Methods of chasing customers

Value of debt

High   Personal visit

                Telephone

                Fax

                E-mail

Low   Letter

Accounts of most importance

- Largest outstanding balances
- Largest arrears
- No recent payments or orders

Letters (Debt collection/Court proceedings/Stop list)

- Address to named individual
- Date
- Sender clearly identified
- Sender signs
- Amount overdue prominently displayed
- Payment by return of post
- Copy letter to purchasing dept
- Specify further actions
- Be prepared to implement threats
- Final letter followed by solicitors' action

Aged receivables' listing | Irrecoverable debts | **Collecting debts**

Telephone

- Have relevant information to hand
- Make sure dealing with right person
- Be formal
- Call at most vulnerable time
- Ensure customer agrees amount and timing of payment
- Know how to deal with excuses

E-mail

- Gives sense of urgency
- Frequent use
- Cannot be diverted
- Not time-consuming

Personal visits

- Time-consuming
- Need appointment
- Confirm agreement in writing

Notes

Notes

Notes

Notes

Notes